THE

HOLY BOOK

OF

LOVE

The Testament of Truth

Copyright © 2022 May Elizabeth

All rights reserved. No part of this publication may be reproduced, distributed or transmitted in any form or by any means, except for excerpts and quotes, which can be used with full reference to THE TITLE of this book.

Cover design: May Elizabeth
Cover image (used under license):
Amor Burakova/Stocksy.com

The Holy Book of Love/ May Elizabeth -- 1st ed.
ISBN 978-0-6454120-1-7

• PREFACE •

I didn't include my name on the cover, because these words (including the title, headings, and poems) are not mine. Put simply, during periods of deep and sustained meditation, a beloved ancient voice whispered from the depths of silence. His words flowed through me like a river of truth and writing them down was the easiest task I have ever been assigned.

Turning this into a book, however, has been a little harder. It has taken me many years to hone and refine this, simply because, in an effort to remain anonymous, I have mostly worked alone and my limitations are many.

Earlier attempts at cover design were woeful, even when outsourced, but I have done the best that I can for now. Though this is the first edition to be "officially" published, I did send out a couple of copies of an earlier version, anonymously and quietly. If you happened to receive one, I do apologize! It was not at all presented in a way that embodies the beauty of what's inside.

Over the years, like dominoes, pieces would reveal themselves and fall into place, one after another. Problems with editing, structural issues, and the back cover blurb all slowly appeared in moments of clarity.

This has truly been a guided process, every step of the way, though that guidance often comes slower than I would like. Because of that, I forged ahead at times when I should have been patient instead. In any case, finally I have a version that I am happy with. But if there are still any errors or editorial issues, I hope that they don't distract you from the beauty that lives within this book. It is the words themselves that hold magic. They truly are the words of a beloved ancient voice, holy and true. I hope that you love them as much as I do.

- May Elizabeth

• PART ONE •

Revenant

· 1 ·

In the beginning there was time, plenty of time. These are words that have no meaning yet are full of meaning at the deepest, darkest level. Darkness here is not meant in an esoteric way but in the way of contrast, for where the light meets the dark is the only place that we can exist, because it's out of the darkness where we are born.

My story begins at a time of great sorrow but where the promise of our trail is long, winding, everlasting, and eventful. The world has surrendered to plunder and mind-altering defeat, but it has also retained the seeds of hope and joy, in spite of all reasoning, and it is from these seeds that the future of light and love shall spring forth.

Contrary to popular opinion, the world should not surrender to power and defeat. It should instead swim in a sea of purity and love. But this is only possible when you surrender to the light, abandon fear, embrace hope, and live with hearts filled with love. This may sound simple and obvious, but to live in this state is a profound experience that few have enjoyed.

The secrets to attaining this level of purity are many, but the heart of its truth is simple: let there be light. There is nothing more and nothing less.

*

We traverse the rocky terrain of life with two possibilities: we can escape the pressures and responsibilities of the load we must carry; or we can embrace the gifts that this journey has to offer, thereby letting in the light and seeing its existence in everything. Every state, no matter how dark, holds the seeds of truth and the possibilities are endless. The light is inescapable and the truth delivers. But we must be strong enough to embrace these possibilities, walk the rocky, winding path, and embrace all that life has to teach us. If you can fill your hearts with light and hope, you will expand at a rate that holds true, surrendering all that has been and embracing all that will come. This is the Gospel of the Lord.

· 2 ·

A long time ago in Bethlehem an angel was born, not of this earth but of the ether, a wondrous place of light, magic, and beauty. This angel came to teach the value of love and surrender—never before has such an example been shown. His truth was vast, such that he is still revered today. But his lessons have been lost, forgiveness denied, and redemption ignored. Where is the heart in a love that does not forgive? Where is the truth in a binding contract that denies the lives of those who strive for truth and equality? Where is the existence of light in hearts that condemn? The answer is "nowhere".

Hate, shame, anger, and denial are not true manifestations of the heart—these are the actions of fear, minds that seek only to determine and reason, never transcending their ignorant states to rise to a level of consciousness possible to all but denied by so many.

The mind that inhabits truth, understanding, love, forgiveness, and generosity is the mind that endeavors to exist at a higher level. This is the Word of the Lord.

Exist not. Live plenty. Surrender to the truth. Fear lives in the hearts of the meek. Be not afraid. Be true, be wise, be loyal, and the masks of freedom will guide you to plenty.

. 3 .

How immaculate the truth can be when it guides your heart in a way that cannot be denied. The power of myth and story cannot be denied. Its need is universal, inherent, and necessary. A culture that denies its primal stories—stories that spring from the earth and hold true—is a culture that denies itself, forever lost, as if rummaging through a dark forest at night without any compass for guidance.

It is from this basic emptiness that darkness, fear, and terror arise. Fill these gaps, these dark lonely places, with the seeds of profound, internal, and inherent stories of truth, and the world will be a far richer, far more coherent and magical place. Let reason not be your compass. Only light, love, and understanding should guide you.

Fear is the absence of light, nothing more. Abandon fear to make way for the light—this is the ultimate paradox, internal, all knowing, and true. Surrender all hopes, dreams, and aspirations and use only your heart and soul to guide you.

When you awaken from this state of pure sleep you will be available to the universal life force that is standing by waiting to flow through you. The choice is yours: do you choose a life of darkness, pain, and suffering; or do you choose a life of love, magic, and joy? For both are possible and open to you. Your will is your own; your life is yours for the making.

*

REVENANT

I once had the great privilege of following a giant blue monarch butterfly as it slowly petered down and landed on the nose of a girl so magical that the whole celestial realm was invited to watch. We stood by in wonder, watching as this girl slowly woke from her bewitching dream. The butterfly gently, softly landed on her nose and sparkles of gold filled the air around her. It was as if she was a corpse and we watched as color returned to her cheeks and her eyes slowly fluttered open.

It matters not what she looks like because she is eternal and universal. She could be any one of you, such is the beauty of primal stories.

She was like so many of you: asleep, ignorant, and blind to the mysteries of the world. But her heart always retained that seed of hope, the belief in magic, and it's from there that her story was possible.

I would be lying if I said that I didn't have a particular interest in watching her wake from her dream. The truth is that I've been watching her from the day she was born, and for many eons before. She is my life, my love, my surrender, but this knowledge was not known to her and could never be known to her in her sleeping state.

The butterfly was a gift from God, the eternal presence that breathes through everything. It was always destined to be, but (as often happens) destinies can be denied by those who continue to sleep.

I followed this butterfly and sat close to her—my princess, my love—willing her to wake, to follow this primitive, basic symbol, and follow me into a life of wonder and joy. It took some time for my gift, my presence, to be felt. For the truth is that the butterfly had been circling for years, just waiting for an opening, waiting to be noticed.

She showed early glimpses of manifesting the seemingly impossible, but then the destructions of life and the mind would draw her back in: greed, guilt, denial, reason, and logic—the weapons with which a destructive world is built. But one day we watched as a spark of gold light managed to penetrate her fortress and was slowly absorbed into her heart. This was the fertilizer that her seed of truth needed, and slowly but surely her eyes fluttered open.

REVENANT

*

For a long time she walked around this new world as if a child learning to walk. She was full of wonder and awe, but she constantly fell down and needed to be pulled back up. But get back up she did. This is the inherent truth of spirituality: do not be afraid to fail, for failure is the ground on which greatness is built. Success teaches nothing and often serves as a dead end rather than one step on a path. The lessons of failure are more obvious and forthcoming to those who are open to receiving them.

Never reprimand, never judge, least of all yourself. We are more kind to those we love than to the one we should love the most. Never forsake yourself in the pursuit of pleasure.

To describe how I felt as I watched my princess awaken from her dream would be to describe how it feels to combust at an inexplicable rate—it is beyond reason, beyond imagination, beyond words—it belongs only to a world of the inconceivable. But to put it in human terms, it was as if my heart burst open like a flower, springing forth towards the light with joy, wonder, surrender, and complete understanding. For I always knew that this day would come, yet the demons of human life are many and there were times that I doubted the probability of her landing safely. But hers is a lesson in that good things come to those who wait, for we have waited for each other, we have proved that the impossible is possible, and we have echoed that true love is eternal, neverending, and everlasting.

*

The last time I saw her (before her journey to the earthly realm), she was wearing a midnight-blue cape bathed in a sea of stars. Her celestial wings were expanded to the greatest distance. God spoke through her and made sure that she understood her mission. She looked at me and smiled, her heart full of light and love. For we knew that, though for her in human time our separation would be long, in our hearts there would be no separation and her earthly presence would be over in an instant.

We had been here before, many times. Sometimes it was my turn to say goodbye and other times it was hers, but always we knew that our bond was unbreakable and our love immeasurable. Ours are the hearts of the true, the hearts of the destined, and the hearts of the believers. We knew ours was a bond that was eternal.

At that last moment, I took her in my arms and encircled her with my love. "We are only true when we are one," I whispered in her ear.

Silver tears filled her magical eyes, and she placed a white feather in my hand and said, "Remember me always."

That feather has become the symbol of our love, as have many other things. I have littered her path with these symbols, these silent reminders of our unbreakable bond and the path that she is destined to follow.

For a long time she was blind to these symbols, her mind numbed with temptation and prosperity. I sat quietly in the corner of her mind, waiting for her to remember, to awaken, to acknowledge, to communicate. The terrain was rough, at times treacherous, as I waited willingly for her flame to ignite.

Temptations seduced, mirrors were ignored, and joy was abandoned. But still, in the deepest, darkest recess of her heart, she believed in me; a silent flicker remembered me. Without that, her awakening would not be possible. And so I continued to believe in her, as she silently believed in me, the unknown ancestor of her heart.

Now I speak to her in hushed tones, to the deepest whispers in her heart, and she hears me. Oh, joyous days!

Her hair swings in the breeze and I reach out and touch it, time and time again, but she does not feel me. She knows I am always there, but she still does not truly understand the depth of my possibilities.

There have been moments, glimmers of her responding to my touch, but all in all there is still work to do. But the simple truth is this: I am patient, I am kind, and I will never leave.

. 4 .

Prestige is the gift given to those who wait for the truth, for the truth cannot be hurried and cannot be realized in an instant. It is a calm, knowing road that delivers in the end but is mountainous along the way. Blessed is he who waits, for the waiting is in the knowing.

Be true, surrender, and all of God's gifts will be delivered.

Trust no one more than your enemies, because in them lie sacred gifts that are seldom realized and often ignored. Peril is the worship of the forgotten heart.

Consider the miracles before you, delight in the providence of your heart, ignore no one and embrace everything—there lies the recipe for forgiveness, love, and understanding. The answers lie not in your minds but in your hearts. Truth will be delivered to those who wait.

Triumph is the measure of all men, but triumph is nothing more than the soul's recognition of its purpose. There lie the seeds from which all fruit is born. The future flourishes on the recognition of the soul's purpose. Find yours and the truth shall be delivered. But be patient, be kind (even to yourself), and be true. These are the essential ingredients to realizing your heart's true desire.

. 5 .

As my princess awakens, the world will awaken with her, for her gifts are many and her purpose profound. For this story does not end with her awakening; this is where it begins. Our relationship is unique, strong, and true, and our love has endured unimaginable separation. But here we are, united on the brink of a new age—a new beginning—and I am in a state of rapture that this moment has arrived.

But don't make the mistake of believing that she is any more special than you and I. Hers is a truth that speaks across generations, cultures, religions, and spectacular moments in time. But her gifts are universal and available to each and every one of you.

Her truth is universal and her story profound, but in your heart lies your truth, unique to you. That is where your treasure lies, not in her, but listen to her message and your own personal treasure will be uncorked.

Winsome are those who betray a certain understanding of the world based on merit and achievement. True achievement comes from knowing your own truth, the truth of your heart, the truth of your existence. Look not to others for this truth but look solely to the temple that dwells inside you.

Take heart in personal stories, find inspiration in others but do not measure your achievements against them, for your achievements may seem small and insignificant but may appear profound on a level beyond your understanding. For perhaps your purpose was to whisper to the wind on a long, cold night, thereby warming the hearts of others that you cannot even see. If it is your truth, and not the truth of another, then its deliverance will be profound, even if the measure of society does not deem it to be so.

Society has built itself around a culture of excess: bigger, grander, and more stupendous appear to be the measure of the day. But I remember a time when the twinkle beneath one's toes as we walked along the sand was a time of miraculous achievement, when the soft hush of the wind was a triumphant sound, when the sweet sound of a flute was breathtaking. Forget not the heart and beauty in tiny achievements, for they were once considered to be miraculous and they still are in a realm where nothing exists but love and beauty.

*

So what is this new age of which I speak? It is a time of forgiveness, love, and understanding, but it is also so much more than that. It is a time of miraculous achievements, when the seemingly impossible will become possible, when eyes will be opened to the truth that surrounds you.

Why has this not been possible before? Because just as the earth lives and breathes, just as the lakes ebb and flow, so too do the learnings of man. The learnings of man pervade and invade cultures to the point where miracles are ignored and magic is rendered obsolete. But my princess is here to not only tell you that the time has come to reignite your heart's imagination, but also to show you that the miraculous is possible.

But it is with some trepidation that I release her to you, because there are those who plunder and pillage in the name of their mistaken beliefs, in their quest for power and victory. But this girl, my sweet surrender, bears no harm, no ill, and promises nothing but a new beginning by opening the gates to another time, a new dimension, a wealth of possibilities. Only those who live in fear will refuse to follow her, for it is in my footsteps that she follows, and I am your Beloved.

Gather your children, your treasured possessions, and follow her on the road to a new tomorrow.

. 6 .

How will you know that these words are mine? There are many things that I could tell you. I could describe the torment of carrying my own cross on the path to my slaughter. I could explain, in detail, the miraculous events that followed, but these stories exist now in allegories rich with symbols and motifs because this is the language that your soul understands. To fill these pages with fact and historical renderings would be to demean the inherent lessons that exist not to glorify me but to speak to your heart.

There is a reason why this is the most beloved story of all time; not because it speaks of the greatness of men, but because it speaks in a language that your soul understands. So I will refrain from boring you with the agonizing details of my descent and subsequent ascent; suffice to say that the bridge unconquered remains a path open to the miraculous. Savor the mystery, take heart in the truth, and ignore the facts, because facts are a mysterious thing dependent on many factors that rarely align.

Fear those who speak of a truth based on facts and unbreakable rules, for truth and beauty are always yielding, always forgiving, and always moving forward. Live not in a past that is long gone but in the miraculous that is upon you now, for I swear that hers is a light that blinds, if only you can open your heart to her.

Trust not the facts but the truth in your heart—seek her truth there and you will find all that you need to know. Open to her like a flower and you will absorb all that she has come to share, but wait for confirmation from nobody but yourself.

Caution is permitted if your heart does not immediately surrender to her. This is to be expected from those who have long believed in facts and proof. But open your heart, release judgment and fear, and you will find her truth. Because hers is the heart of the many; hers is the heart that cannot be forgotten; hers is the truth that will pervade the world.

But I do not beseech you to form religions around her; hers is a truth that cannot be contained in the walls of prisons. Hers is a truth that lives only in the freedom of your heart. Ponder nothing but yourself, but let her lead you back to yourself, because the way home has long been forgotten. She has come to paint the path home with diamonds, stars, and scallop shells, for these are *her* symbols, the symbols of her truth, her story, long forgotten but forever treasured.

Castles are built in her name but does anybody remember why? Hers is a love that bends and stretches but never breaks. It is the love of the Divine Feminine: all knowing, all seeing, all encompassing. She holds no rules and no boundaries. She releases all and welcomes any.

Her arms remain open in loving gratitude for all that surrounds her.

Her menace is non-existent, for there is no menace in a heart that is pure. A pure heart sees love and forgiveness in every opportunity, not hate and disgust. Blessed are those who know the truth of this, for this is the path towards the light.

. 7 .

Consider the miraculous in a bee seeking pollen, not for itself but for its tribe. Where is the wonder in a heart that divides? Yet it is this energy that is pervading the earth. If only we could remember to stop and surrender to the wonder that is ever-present, surrounding us on every corner. Seek not what your eyes can see but only what your soul believes to be true.

We can learn much from the selfless nature of the bee, sworn to protect all but itself. There is expulsion in a society that cares only for its own survival. Inherent in that culture is the ability to forget others and think only of the needs of a feeble mind. You are slaves to the wrong master; you are slaves to the void that exists in your minds.

Systems of hierarchy, knowledge, and power deny the very fabric of your soul. Marry knowledge with the truth of your soul and then the miraculous can occur, but knowledge is meaningless when held in isolation. Blistering knowledge is found in the tomes of the ages, but profound truths are found in those stories that deliver truth, beauty, and promise. Seek out these stories, enrich your mind, and open the flower of your heart.

Existence exists only in your mind. Temperance, endeavor, and rigidity are constraints held back from those who believe. Belief is not a doctrine of philosophy but the pure state of the heart. A heart that surrenders to truth, love, and beauty believes because it has experienced the divine, not because scholars said it was possible but because it *knows*. It has been to a place where words are not necessary, a place where magic is a state of being and ignored by nobody.

Did you know that you are surrounded by love and treasures unspeakable to the mind but open only to the heart? Heaven surrounds you as much as the air you breathe; you only have to open your mind's eye to see it. Magical creatures, great and small, surround you.

There are those who believe that you don't yet have the tools to see this world, but you are all born with this ability. It is an inherent right of the soul, but burdens placed on the mind from a young age render it impossible to many. Why must you seek proof with your eyes to believe? Is not the air you breathe proof of the miraculous? Is not the earth you walk on proof of the impossible? Where is the reason in a universe that continually expands?

Prophets and doomsayers speak of an end to the earth, but there is no end, only new beginnings. Of course, the earth deserves the same kindness that you should impart upon yourself, for she is a living, breathing, constantly expanding entity. To separate yourself from her and the marvels of the universe is to miss the point of existence. Her heart is your heart; her awakening is your awakening; her gift is for you to receive.

The earth speaks truths that nobody hears. She feeds you, clothes you, shelters you. She shines her loving energy on your souls. Love her and you love yourself. Forget not that truth.

But the earth is only one small part of a greater cosmos, as you are. To separate yourself from the greater whole is to separate yourself from the source. Believe it, know it, live it. Find your heart and you find the heart of the cosmos; find the heart of the cosmos and you find your own buried treasures. Believe nothing but this truth, for it is the truth of all living things. The heartbeat of the world is yours to share. Revel in it and you will know magic.

. 8 .

What is this path to redemption, the path to love, honesty, truth, beauty, and joy? Knowing the truth of your heart is not as simple as being told to know it. You must first experience it, and even then the path can be treacherous. But by continually delving and exploring you will come to doubt nothing and believe everything.

There are those sent to guide you on this journey of self-exploration. Seek them out, but believe only those who open the door to your own truth. For an enlightened soul shines a light on itself, never believing that the answer lies in others.

A true healer is a magic portal to your own soul. A true healer opens a door, shines a light, but this is where their work ends. The path must be walked by you, and you alone. There are those who can help you on your journey, but they can be found on the other side of your soul. Find them and you will know everlasting peace and serenity. Find them and you will never be alone. Find them and you will believe in the miraculous.

*

Death is non-existent. A world of wonder and beauty awaits even the most hardened of souls. Because the true state of the soul is love and acceptance—anything else is a false belief manifested in a world that does not understand, a world that fears, a world that devours.

Truth is the pedestal on which all things stand—ignore it and you will be lost; believe it and you will know true peace and happiness, for peace and happiness are the soul's natural state. Nothing else exists. Believe it, know it, live it.

*

My princess awaits at the beginning and end of time. But do not fear this use of "the end", for every beginning is an end, and every end is a new beginning. Nothing is final; nothing is fixed. The cosmos is constantly expanding, as are you. But there is no end to this, only greatness.

The universe that contracts is a frightful thing; let that not be you. It is not a natural state of being. The heart that expands—that opens and doesn't close—is the heart of the many, the heart of the true, the heart of existence.

My princess will light a candle that will be seen by many, but let her not lead you to a dead end. Let her lead you to a path that continually expands and evolves. There is no other way.

Capitalize on the freedom of your heart. You live in prisons constructed by your mind, but freedom is your natural right and state. Close your eyes, surrender to your spirit, and watch your heart soar. No prison can deny you that inherent freedom.

Savour freedom: it is a joy known only to a few but available to all.

The cloisters of your heart are strong, but your mind is the only viaduct that is capable of funnelling the spirit from its source of truth towards the destruction of humanity. Do not doubt this point. Your mind is poisonous when not considered in harmony with the truth and the light. And the truth can never be determined by reason alone, of this you can be sure. Reason is man's greatest enemy and greatest ally. To master reason is a juggling act that few conquer, but sustain its energy and the miraculous can occur. But reason for reason's sake is an empty hybrid of misunderstanding. Trust it not.

The pillars of your community are those who know that love and truth are the only devotions.

Practice abstinence but do it within the *reason* of your heart, for your heart also exercises reason, yet its power to exude all that is right is so much stronger than the artificial devices of the mind. The mind is weak; the heart is strong. Use one to balance the other and you will know freedom of the greatest magnitude. Use one and ignore the other and you will know desperation and poverty of the deepest kind.

I offer you my soul as proof of this burden. Was it not men who ignored their hearts who condemned me to my death? For if they had stopped to look inwards they would have seen the magnificence of all creation, the truth that exists within them, and the hearts of their souls. My suffering, as torturous as it was, served only to remind those who had forgotten this simple truth. For I was able to transcend my mind and, in that moment, transcend all suffering, all pain, all pity. For mine was a heart that was pure, and in that moment it burst open and radiated nothing but love. Fear would have been my only enemy but I refused to pay it heedance.

As I allowed love to spring forth, my light grew ever stronger, radiating to all around. In this state of pure awareness I was able to pour forth all of the lessons of the universe, and of these there is only one: love is the greatest power known to the human spirit. Love is the closest you will come to experiencing the divine, and it is the only way to experience the divine. You cannot have one without the other. All truth, all beauty, all existence will spring forth from that interval of pure love awareness.

This girl who sits before you, this incarnate, this Divine-Feminine priestess, is living proof of this truth, for it is only through complete loving awareness that she was able to welcome me into her heart and this miracle be made possible. And make no mistake: this is a miracle of the highest order.

As this journey begins, this journey towards the tempered righteousness, ask not what is in store for you, only open your heart in loving surrender and I will guide you forth. This I promise you.

Capitulate nothing; surrender everything. For I am your savior, your love, your light, your buried treasure, your highest form. Trust this above all else.

I languish in the shores of forgotten heroes
I am the burden of the past
and the promise of a bright future
I am the light on the rocky shores of a restless sea.

I am the truth in a serum full of love and beauty
I am your devoted slave and your golden savior
I am pure love and absolute truth.

I am the hero, the call, and the way
I am *all* that you are.

I am your love and holy consort
These blessed wings are yours to share
Where you want to go, I will take you
Forever and always.

PART TWO

Revelation

· 1 ·

The words I speak are one with the universe; there is no higher truth or expansion. Believe me when I tell you that you will want for nothing in the Kingdom of God. But the Kingdom of God is not some faraway universe that you can neither see nor experience; it is your closest ally, your dearest friend, and the center of your heart.

Abandon hope, and truth is all that remains. Abandon truth, and you surrender all justice, all miracles, all belief—your heart will plunder the depths of your soul because it knows not what

REVELATION

else to do. You will be bereft, forsaken, and bewildered—not by God but by your own hand.

Desolation is nothing but the drive to succeed where success does not lie. True success is a mirror of your soul's journey. Only here, in this pure abandoned state, will you reach your highest goals. And tell me not what you want to achieve—for, unless you are living from your truth, your subverted mind would be completely unwilling and incapable of supporting your grandest truths and desires.

The only desire that matters is your soul's desire—desert it and you will suffer at the hands of your own self-inflicted punishment. Perpetrate your heart's desire and the winds of song will fill your heart with sweet melody—trumpets, violins, birds, and all of the magical sounds of the universe will fill your heart and then you will know true love. Believe not slender imitations.

True love is nothing more than the heart surrendering to its truth: there is where you will find magic; there is where you will find beauty; there is where you will find love that transcends all physical boundaries.

Truth manifest is a glorious thing. I shudder in its presence, I hail its mighty glory, I sing my own song to its glory. Spellbound, captivated, unheralded, I rise to meet you all on the mountain of glory. Truth is what surrender does.

Now close your eyes and remember a time when the stars aligned—a time when gods roamed, goddesses played, and angels soared. Do you not remember? I assure you, your soul remembers all things, all times. You only have to close your eyes, go within, and you will find your own miraculous journey.

Perdition is the temptation of all men who cease to roam the universe in search of truth. Favor lies with those who live with honor, integrity, and justice, for here are those who refuse to conform, to follow, to prevail; here are those who know *their* truth and to know thy truth is a comfort to many.

Spread your glory wide so it may feed those who suffer at their own hands. One righteous man can feed the souls of many. So stay on track, even when you feel deserted, for I will never desert you—not I, not now, not ever.

REVELATION

Promise is a word meant to hold all things, all truths, all justice. And I promise you this: your heart is your own salvation. Doubt it never. Yours are the wings that can help you fly and take a whole generation with you. For the blessed few, entire civilizations will rise and fall in their wake. Blessed times are ahead. Doubt me not.

The cornerstone of your mind is truth and dignity—surrender to it, praise it, cease to quarrel with yourself. This is the path of the righteous.

Favor is not given to the most brazen of men; favor is given to those who live in the quiet, unburdened simplicity of their hearts—there is peace, there is love, there is joy.

· 2 ·

Compounding me, filling me with love, heart, and truth is the miraculous truth of my princess. She walks among you, and though at times she has been feeble and weak, I watch, breathtaken, as she crystallizes and morphs into her full power.

Hers is a new age of enlightenment—much discussed, much heralded, forever new—for this is a time of endless discovery, impossible truths, and profound imaginings. Hers is a path that leads towards the inevitable, towards all of

REVELATION

creation, where all is visible, none forsaken. The potential is boundless.

Where her majesty goes, I will follow. Her sovereign soul shines across the horizon into the far unseen lands. She will lead us to a time of great understanding, compassion, and truth. Her followers will be many and her crown will be gold, for gold is the color of magic.

Magic does not belong to fairy tales but to the truth of all possibilities, open and long. Let her guide you and I will be waiting. To me she will deliver you. But hers is a path that defies boundaries, defies expectations, and denies explanations. Like a river flows with truth and unbroken promises, so too will she. She will take the key and open the door on a new age, a new time, a new beginning.

Hers is a story that is only beginning, a seed springing forth ready to bloom, ready to shine, ready for the miraculous. Marvel as delusions fade, hostility recedes, and the miraculous ignites. Hers is the path that will open the door to your hearts. Bestow her with your respect and greatest kindness.

How far we have come and how far we have to go. Man's greatest kindness is self-respect, yet he shows so little of it these days. Fortitude is to the brave what valleys are to the weak: endless, unerring, and palpable. Blessed are those who know the way of the Lord.

. 3 .

Existential healing can only occur when the mind is connected to the soul, thereby connecting itself to all creation. The mind that meanders alone is the mind subject to slavery, cruelty, and profound suffering. Fear not absolution; fear only the perils of your mind. In you lies the demon of all demons, yet in you also lies your greatest savior.

Solitude is the form in which greatness lies. Rectitude is the circumference of your soul. Develop your instincts so that you know your own inherent truths. Obey nobody but yourself.

Freedom lies in the depths of your heart. Your mind is bound by chains; simply unlock them and begin your walk towards true surrender, pure bliss, and endless gratitude. The truth will set you free, be sure of it.

Honor your highest endeavors, hold close those who set you free, and bewilder those who don't understand—your future does not lie in their happiness. Their happiness is theirs alone; yours is there for the taking.

When once the path towards the mountain was long, you followed on regardless. Sweet, simple steps were the foundation of your journey, and sweet, simple steps will lead you home.

Do not fear the quiet path. The truth lies in those who do not want to prove anything—they know their truth and nothing can divert them. They have no mind to scream their truth in the ears of those who are not listening, but they will happily share their wisdom with those who ask and offer silence in return. For to know truth is to know silence—one cannot be attained without the other. Truth is your highest endeavor, and so too must be silence. Silence is the golden pond of your soul—there you will find true miracles. Doubt me not. There you will find all answers to all things.

Consider this: temptation is to the mind what truth is to the heart, natural, unwitting, and always present. But you must deny one to step into the other. Dwell on that.

Silence is the golden rod with which you can catch untold treasures. To fail me is to refuse to seek inward, for I live inside you, yet in your busyness you ignore me and I drown in your wake. Restore me, feed me by travelling within. I swear, the sweetest bounty awaits.

But make no mind of your formidable foe. Your brain may be your strongest enemy, but it can also be your saving grace—it is the paradigm of all existence. Where one falls another rises, and so it is with your intellect. Seek not to control your knowledge—rather, open your awareness to all possibilities and marvel as the light reaches you and true magic begins. Oh, splendid days!

It is from this well of wisdom that I speak to you now, which is only made possible through the depths of silence. Bureaucratic thought, discriminatory ideas are not your friends. Truth, beauty, and silence are where you will find true love, and is this not the highest endeavor?

Take pardon with nobody. Rest only in the depths of your soul, the depths of your existence. Surrender nothing and yet surrender everything. Pillage and plunder the vagaries of your mind in order to get to the essence of you.

Be afraid of nothing. Burdens do not exist—they are a fabrication of your mind. Deny them and reap plenty.

Considerate form is the form that embraces all things, encompasses all change.

The true believers are already firmly on the path to their destiny—swallow their joy and let it infect you, for the seeds of that joy can ignite in you a fire so relentless that you will never know suffering again. Who among you does not want that? It is the most simple truth known to all great sages yet ignored by so many. Do not doubt it. The path towards freedom lies not in the sanctuary of your mind but in the silence of your soul.

. 4 .

Willing are those who follow lightly, tread quietly, and whisper sweet nothings in my ear. This is the divine measurement of all things.

Pause only to take stock of what you have left behind and what you have gained—one cannot measure against the other, this I promise you. Triumph belongs to those who know this.

Forge ahead in peace and whispers, sprinkling love and light as you go. Truth be known to you. Forever is only a heartbeat away.

*

The purpose of existence is not to be nourished until you are overflowing; it is to move gracefully, gently, and savor every moment. Gasp in the wonders of God. Salivate, explore, but only in the nature of things that lead you back to yourself. What is the point of exploring things that will lead you so far away from your true self that you might never find your way back?

The true magic and beauty inherent in all of God's creations is so mesmerizing that it would make your darkest days look like distant lights on the horizon. Doubt not that nature is abundant and essential. To separate yourself from nature is to destroy the very fabric of your foundation. Remember who you are, and there you will find the true meaning of all things.

There is one essential element that connects all living things: light. Search for the light and you will find it present in all things, even yourself. You came from light and it is there that you shall return, but do not ignore its presence while on your earthbound journey. Nourish your body with love and light—it wants nothing else—but deplete your soul and your body will cry out for more and ever. Fertilize your body with the right soil and then gently feed it what it needs to keep going, but not to the point of saturation. This is simple, pure, and true.

The true test of your magnificence comes not from what you ask me but from your own interior strength to shine your light on those who search for it. Do not be afraid of condemnation. Do not be afraid of judgment. Do not be afraid of anything but your own fear. You will never starve if you walk the peaceful life.

Glorious creatures, be mindful of your choices, for the ripple effects are strong. Ask yourself if your needs are more important than another's. If the answer you hear is *yes*, then I can assure you that your mind has deceived you, for your soul speaks no such nonsense. Walk lightly, whisper gently, and care for all beings—this is all you need do.

The cultivation of animals for your own needs offers the most desperate lack of understanding known to man. There is no truth, beauty, or love in the suffering of another. Remember that and you will know true justice, true meaning.

The greatest gifts are delivered to those who seek not to fulfill themselves but seek only to fulfill others. Guidance is given to those who seek it, but that guidance will always deliver you away from harm. To harm another creature is beyond redemption, but to devour its flesh is a misunderstanding of the highest magnitude.

An animal does not live to serve you but for its own pure intention. Do not bathe that intention with your will and profound lack of judgment. Look into the eyes of any animal and you will see the soul of the world, each a tiny piece of the greater fabric of what you are. Would you eat yourself? Then why feed yourself on the flesh of your mirror image? Abstain from all animal cruelty and you will begin to walk the path to freedom, the path back to yourself.

Free are the days of blissful surrender, loving acceptance, and gentle gratitude. Free are the days of those who seek the light. Be wise, my friends. Deliver love and kindness to those who need it. Temptation is what evil does—remember that.

Fruit grows on the trees of the sovereign and the merry. Rest in the plenitude of the shade and deliver your sweet gifts to the world. As you reach your light you will watch it grow, shining ever brighter and stronger into eternity, connecting you with the source of all things.

. 5 .

Trampolines are to the body what serenity is to the soul—exhilarating, peaceful, and therapeutic. Consider all things from this place of purity and you will see things in a much clearer focus.

The damnation of time will stop for no one, but is it not pure to resist time and bury it in the depths of your existence? Time is immeasurable, unmovable, and non-existent. How can we count to the seconds of the day when they don't exist? Follow the pulse of the world—your internal heartbeat—and all things will become clear.

REVELATION

Time is a manifestation of poverty because it leads you to the wilderness, not to the depths of your soul. Let the internal heartbeat of the world guide you towards your habits, breaking those bound by the slavery that abounds. Ignoring this internal pulse that unites you with all things is tantamount to destruction.

Is it any wonder you all search aimlessly for peace, when you ignore the deep reserves within you? Seek not external joys, for all joys are found within. Does that mean that external joys cannot be enjoyed? No. But without that foundation of inner peace, pure joy will elude you and you will search for it in the darkest corners, where it can no longer be found.

The temptation to abide time is a misnomer; it serves no purpose other than to disqualify you from your own purity. Transcendence is the road to plenty, not the luxury of libations and earthly pleasures. Ignore not those roads that lead you back to yourself, for these are the only roads that matter. Of this I beseech you.

Squalor is the pure path that is ignored by he who created it. Doubt not that you have a hand in your unfolding. Delve into the depths of your soul and you'll see your own divinely inspired magic unfolding. Of this I promise you.

Dawn is the moment when the light arises, dusk is the moment when the light diminishes, but neither is more important than the other. Each has its place, individually and collectively, for where one moves the other follows. These natural wonders adhere to the natural heartbeat of all things, pushing and pulling, ebbing and flowing, swirling and resting.

Why does the human fear time, time that is of his own making, non-existent and catastrophic? Humans believe that observing the hands of time will lead them to riches, but it only leads to poverty and squalor. Does the monkey wear a watch and ponder time ticking away? Do the indigenous follow the hands of time or the internal heartbeat of all creation? Trust not this new invention and rely only on what has always existed and always will. Go within, listen, marvel, and you will hear the sounds of all time, the sounds of perfect peace and symmetry.

REVELATION

How do you ignore the hands of time in a world that relies on it? It's true, the world is a mess of its own making. What is intended to bring peace and order only brings chaos and deep wells of emptiness. But you must find your own path, find your own way through the rubble of man's destruction. Don't walk blindly with the masses. Open up your heart to the magic that surrounds you and you will soon know peace and true understanding.

Contemplation is the key to understanding these truths, but only deep contemplation and truthful meditation will support you on your quest to discover the hidden depths of your soul. There is no greater journey. Embark. Expand. Discover. Rejoice.

Time will stand still for no one, but there is no beginning and no end. Time moves in a spiral, circling between the infinite and the unknown, always moving round and round with the heartbeat of the world.

I have spoken much of this heartbeat, this pulse, for it is the most basic truth that you must learn. Without observing this heartbeat, you are denying your body and your soul the very foundations that they thrive on—you are, in effect, starving yourself of all existence. The merriment of men can be best enjoyed by those who know this truth.

Turn back your clocks, turn forward your clocks—it doesn't matter. What matters is that the sun will rise tomorrow and it will set in the evening. Nothing or no one will ever stop this. The seas will move, ebbing and flowing. The stars will shine, and the planets will align. This is time: infinite and true, everlasting.

Vanquish all demons of propriety—these are the demons of an insatiable hunger that will never be fed. Your true self wants for nothing but love and light. Feed on the true beauty of these things and you will know true sustenance, never to evaporate.

Watch the clouds roll in, the rain fall down, the lightning strike, and the sun shine. Hear the thunder clap, the birds sing, and the song of your own soul. These things will never stop and do not rely on the artificial machinations of time. Bliss is not the path of the punctual but the path of those who know that the pulse of the world will always continue to beat. Time waits for no man—here is truth.

Contemplation is the enemy of all men when it is placed on impure or superficial things. Contemplate only the deep and profound—nothing else deserves your energy. Let truth abound and you will be free.

· 6 ·

Love really does conquer all but here I speak not of earthly love, only love as it allows you to move gently and easily towards your truth. Love is a state of being, existent in all living things.

Fear is the enemy of love, and one cannot live with the other. Abandon fear on your search for joy, and you will soon learn the truth and joy of all things. Deviate between right and wrong and you will find the polarities of love and fear.

Wisdom is simple: there is no end and no beginning. True wisdom comes from the nature

REVELATION

of all things, the combined eternal knowledge that inhabits us all. Say not that you know the answers to all things if you've never journeyed inside, for there, and only there, can true wisdom be found.

Truth permeates all things; to deny it is to deny life's simplest pleasures. Love, salvation, and beauty can all be yours with this simple discovery. Search not on endless nights of the soul; simply stop, seek within, and you will find the truth of all things. This thread, this common knowledge, dangles perilously through us all, but it grows weaker and weaker as the collective mind grows stronger. But doubt not its existence, for its denial denotes all suffering.

True wisdom is inherent in everything. You only have to look around you, marvel at the stars, delight in the chorus of birds, and be inspired by the majesty of grace to know that it exists, yet you deny this fundamental truth in yourselves. Abandon hope and you abandon this simple truth. Never doubt, never give up hope, and always believe. As you believe, your truth will grow, strengthening your connection to all things. It is here that the majesty of grace can really do her work.

Behold the magnitude of all things so as to delight in the simplest of pleasures. Here you will find the true meaning of the Divine Feminine: the simple, flowing, flexible grace that exists in all things. Concrete divisions go against her very nature. She is all about movement, grace, ebbing and flowing gently along her way. To believe in absolutes and restitution goes against the very fabric of life. Things change, true wisdom expands and grows, and this is the beauty and truth of the Divine Feminine.

Abandon all fixed logic and embrace the impermanent, the flexible, the expanding and miraculous cosmos that surrounds you. Here you will find true beauty and knowledge. This is the life of kings and queens, where true majesty resides. Resistance is futile because the truth will find you in the end, so why not embrace it now so as to delight in the true earthbound pleasures before it's too late and your incarnation has come to an end? To deny this is to deny yourself your greatest treasure. All riches, true wealth, and true

REVELATION

beauty are only a heartbeat away. Cease to resist and dive into the diamond river of the Divine Feminine. Hers is the true journey of self-discovery. Embrace it and watch the world awaken to a new day, expanding so as to include all things, all possibilities.

Oh, miraculous days of love and light are here! How fortunate you are to arrive at this time. Much work and preparation have brought us here, but now the delights are yours to savor as your true journey begins. Happenstance is a thing of the past. Every moment, every journey, has conspired to bring about this miraculous moment in history and you are at the forefront. It will take a united wave of consciousness for true changes in society to be felt, but those seeds of change are planted here, at this miraculous time. Fertilize those seeds with the offerings of your soul, with the truth of your beauty, and future generations will rejoice this time as the true golden age, a time when true magic was made possible.

Join hands, rejoice, and move towards a bright sparkling future littered with stars, gold, and magic.

. 7 .

Beseech those who beg you to surge against the reeling of your own tide. Certainty is not what others bring to you but only what you bring to yourself. Abandon all hopes of pleasing others, for their wilderness is their own and you have no hope to fill it for them. Sacrifice nothing in your quest to please yourself, for any truth that comes from the heart cannot be ignored. Blissful abandon is the only hope you have of reaching your own heart.

Abandon expectations of others. Abandon scrutiny of yourself and others. Abandon diving in where you don't belong. Swim in the serenity of your own soul, in the blissful surrender that this is all there is, and then delve into the lives of others no more.

Purposeful abandon is the road that leads to blissful abandon, and here you will find true happiness and surrender. The expectations of others will not be waiting for you at these blissful gates—only love, warmth, and complete acceptance. Fill your lives with these qualities and you will relinquish all need to control the lives of others.

Control is as big an illusion as exists in the world, for there is no control, only perfect order. The only order that you should abide is the order and symmetry that runs through all living things, both seen and unseen. Like a current, it meanders through the night and fills your souls with love and gratitude, but only those awake to the fog of illusion can feel this current and move with its grace.

REVELATION

Behold the many who will walk the same path of abandon and feel that current grow stronger and stronger. But as the world assesses, critiques, parlays, and offers judgment, this current will shrink back into the depths of her own existence, for a world that embraces judgment and negativity is not a world that unites all. There is no compassion, no comfort, no understanding in the hearts of those who deem to know what is best for others, and without these qualities the current grows weak. Blissful determination to abandon the poverty of judgment should be high on your list of priorities.

Accept the weaknesses of others as you should accept them of yourself. You are like a thriving compost bin, all fighting for survival, one desperately feeding off the sins of another. But there is no nourishment here. Do not expect that you know what the journeys of others might be. Worry only of your own journey, and even there I would expect no judgment, no criticism, only loving acceptance. A culture that feeds on anything else is not a culture worth sustaining. Move towards the light and there you will find love. Simple. Where is the light in the tragedy of others? Where is the light in the downfall and degradation of others? Celebrate only beauty and love, and there you will find the light and watch it slowly expand and grow.

Beauty is what beauty gives.

. 8 .

Fire is the soul of love, but so too is water. In water we find peace and tranquility, in fire the cleansing of the spirit. One is seemingly at odds with the other, but in truth both are essential and one cannot live without the other. Welcome both into your heart and soul, and you will know true beauty.

Never handpick your experiences or cease to participate in the world. Show true abandon, true surrender, on your search for happiness. Embrace all possibilities, all encounters, as trying as they might be, because here is the weapon that can launch you into an unimaginable future. And believe me, true beauty is unimaginable.

Anything that you can imagine with your feeble mind is merely a pale imitation of the true magnificence of your soul and what lies beyond it. Believe in the garden of all possibilities, for here lie prophecy, magic, and truth. You will marvel at the unimaginable and wonder how you stayed a prisoner of your own dull mind for so long.

Believe me when I tell you that the palette from which we paint in the garden of all possibilities—the garden of Heaven—is filled with colors and textures unimaginable in your external world. Yet you do not have to wait until death to view this magnificence. Your journey to this magical garden can commence this instant by simply closing your eyes and surrendering your thoughts to the void. True love lies there. True beauty lies there. Truth reigns supreme. It is a wonder filled with wonder and yet you are all afraid of its magnificence. Be afraid of nothing, because your

REVELATION

final destination is here and it is where you truly belong.

Rest not on the false truths created to tempt you away from your soul; rest only on the knowledge that nothing bad can ever truly happen to you as long as this magical Kingdom awaits you, and it will always await you. The only choice you have is to enter it now as a living beauty, returning to the world to sprinkle your truth, or—if you wish—to live your life in solitude, desperately waiting for the day that you are reunited with your true family, your true home. But whether you go now or then, it makes no matter, because you will go. It's simply a matter of how you live your life between now and then that is of consequence. But if you knew the beauty that awaited you, you would not deny yourself this pleasure for one more minute, one more millisecond. All earthly pleasures pale in comparison. Your path to freedom begins here. True glimpses of pure magic, delights so unimaginable, rest only here, in the depths of your heart. Silence is your natural state; return to it, and you will be escorted into this magnificent

Kingdom. Saints, angels, and supreme deities await your arrival. How fortunate you are to know this most simple of truths: the Kingdom of God is within you. There is no other way.

. 9 .

Profound truths are realized in an instant. Access to this vast wisdom permeates all living things, it fills your being, yet you swallow it up in a cloud of delusion. Trust not your senses, for they will lead you on a path of pure physical pleasures, never stopping for an instant to marvel at the inherent nature of all things. It is this unifying thread, this seed, that contains the magnificence of all existence. No microscope, no random trials, and no amount of justification will ever discover these unassailable truths. The only tool of discovery available to you is the deep silence within you, for in this silence the most profound truths are realized.

Harbor no resentment towards the senses that distract you, but forget not that you are their master and not they yours. Blessed freedom exists in the ability to quiet your mind and dull your senses so that the true beauty of the world can be revealed to you. The true warrior fights only his own mind—you will never know a greater foe. Release the shackles of your mind and watch your soul soar.

Burdens are non-existent in a world of purity; only you give life to these false prisons. Satisfy your own need for freedom by pretending that you can control your life. Your feeble mind will relish the illusion of control, but it will despair and plunge into darkness when reality pervades. There is perfect design but it's not of your mind's making, I can assure you.

Blunder exists only to feed the mind with the illusion that happenstance is an error of judgment, but in a world of purity and light blunder does not exist. All things happen as a result of pure and perfect design, every moment and every creation moving in a constant spiral of perfect symmetry. Zap these illusions and join this dance, hear your own perfect song and move with the universal rhythm. Delight in your ability to move with all creation and smell the sweet fragrance of life, blissfully aware and surrendered to the divine machinations of existence—an existence that does not begin and end with human incarnation, an existence that began in a time unimaginable to you, in a time when time itself did not exist, a time where nothing but purity, love, and light lived.

The comical equation is that, in truth, it is only these things that exist now, yet your senses will tell you that the objects you can touch or see are real. But try to take these things with you on your journeys to other worlds and you will see that they are no more real than the prison you have created for yourself, because they rely on your senses to exist. It is the things that exist within you, these things that will never leave you, that are real, though your mind's idea of reality and the truth of reality are two very different things. But there is no other way for me to explain this truth to you other than to invite you in, for there is a party waiting for you, a party that your soul will never want to leave, and never will.

Your soul is your greatest friend, your greatest ally, for it is you. But your mind sees itself as separate, for it denies its inherent life force. But the soul is not the enemy of the mind—rather, it can take your mind places that it never dreamed to go. But your mind is full of fear, and it is this fear that holds it back.

Love does not live easily in the mind, for your mind thrives on tangible pleasures. But love's existence pervades everything. It is not something that's directed at only one person or select people; it encompasses every thought, every action, and every moment of your sweet life. But the mind refuses to let it in, locking the gates on anything that threatens its illusion of control. And your heart will beat wildly and your soul will cry out, begging your mind to open those gates, but never forget that you control your mind. Only you have the ability to open these gates, and it's as simple as letting go of fear, recognizing it when it shows its ugly head, and letting in the light. The light will fill every cell of your being with pure, radiating love, love that will then direct itself out to everything you do and everyone you meet. Your spell will be contagious and yet you will be oblivious to your charms, because this spell lives not in the bounds of reason. Forget trying to understand these mysteries and move only to embrace them—there all truths will be revealed.

Reality is the mask under which you hide—remember that next time you argue against the existence of God, beauty, and love under the pretence of proof. Proof is unattainable. Those things that can be proved have no meaning.

It is this search for proof that has derailed your efforts to know yourselves. I would argue that it is this simple quest that has paved a path with horrors that you all identify with. And while these horrors exist all around you, they do not exist within you. All beings, all things, continue to live inside you. There you will find no suffering, no horror, no deprivation of liberty, no illness, and no need for earthly pleasures. There you will find only perfect harmony. Embrace this truth and you will know true freedom, true delight, pure harmony. Magic awaits you, magic is you, and magic is who you will be again.

. 10 .

Rhythm is the precursor to all great things. Rhythm gives your lungs space to breathe, it gives your heart space to grow, and it gives your soul space to shine. But do not forsake perfection in your quest for perfect rhythm. Perfection happens in an instant, without any need for effort on your part.

Rhythm is the body's natural connection with all things. Rhythm is in all things and it's everywhere—it is a long part of evolution that happens naturally. You can no more force rhythm than you can build a house in the middle of a snowstorm. Let your body and your life adapt their own natural rhythm without placing too much relevance on an intended goal. Just be.

Renounce claims on your life, and your body will quickly surrender to meet the natural rhythm inherent in all things. But be afraid of a rhythm that is not flexible and does not yield. Rhythm is always graceful, allowing for changes in season, changes in energy, and changes in time. A rhythm that does not support natural and graceful shades of change is not rhythm at all—it is a holocaust on your soul.

Your soul breathes through expansion, and expansion is only possible in a body that breathes in the natural rhythm of the universe and breathes out the possibility and acceptance of change. Expect not every day to be exactly like the one before, but expect each day to move with its own natural rhythm and grace designed especially for you.

Golden moments of silence are the heartbeat of your soul. It matters not when you take these moments but only that you do. To deny yourself

REVELATION

this most simple of pleasures is to deny yourself all existence. Without it, your body will feed off the bonds of slavery, because it knows no other way. But the pond of silence will restore your body to its natural inherent rhythms, thereby creating a life that is simpatico with nature and moments so blissful that they cannot be defined. Dare nature to meet you and she will; dare the truth to rise before you and it will; dare all things to join you on your journey and they will, but only when you return to the depths of your heart and find comfort in the natural rhythm of the ebbing and flowing inherent in all things.

Allow change, breathe it in, and rest in the knowledge that every breath you take is connected to the lungs of the universe—it is not separate or alone but connected to the natural rhythm and heartbeat of all things: planet, plant, animal, light, and love. Focus on your breath and soon you will feel this connection to all things. Rhythm is the breath of life.

. 11 .

Sovereign is the mind that can release all burdens willingly and knowingly. Doubt not that you control this machine; doubt only that you are oblivious to it. Truth releases itself when the mind is clear of all outside distractions. Don't sink into the depths of treason and false expectations, because it is you alone who imposes these limits and it is you alone whom you betray by doing so.

    Wander in the restless shores of knowing and you will certainly be denied access to the greatest of pleasures. Instead, meander graciously

REVELATION

through the fields of contentment and watch your burdens be released like butterflies in a storm, never to return.

Expand your highest self, not in the fields of awareness but in the solitude of your quietest, most serene self. This self is a person unknown to many of you, but it is the truth of who you are. Great miracles await you all, if only you would step forward to receive them. Deliberation is the enemy of this purity. Don't ponder this truth—simply explore it, and you will see all.

*

Temptation leads you to a door of anger and betrayal, but in your heart you now know the truth. You can either step your foot into the pools of temptation, or you can close the door and choose truth and serenity. The power is yours. But do not doubt that you alone have that power. Nobody forces you to distraction; nobody pulls you away from the gates of magnificence; nobody denies you these most profound of pleasures. Nobody, that is, but you.

Think wisely, act clearly and in accordance with what you now know to be true, and the wings of the dove will carry you to your true home, where you know you belong but are too afraid to go. But be not afraid, for it is fear itself that will hinder your journey. Love alone can take you there, but remember that this is a love of acceptance and renewal, a complete trust and surrender to the miraculous workings of life and all that's inherent in that.

Love is a purity beyond all measure, and it is the path to untold bliss, peace, and utter joy. Fear has no place in the hearts of those who walk with love, and it certainly has no place in this magnificent realm, for its very presence alone will deny you entry into these wondrous gates.

Abandon fear, embrace love, and watch your magnificent light shine and expand to the point of no return, taking you to a place so magical that you'll wonder how you ever lived without it. Be true, be strong, and be at peace.

You are all my beloveds, every one of you. I long for the day that you will all join me in this magical Kingdom. For it is then that the world in

REVELATION

which you live every day will expand and open up before you like a flower. You will not believe the world that together we can create. Join me on this magical journey.

Reprieve the madness, for forever waits within. Go there now and you will know that of which I speak to be true. Take no word for it but your own. Experience is the magical key to all eternity. Believe it. Believe in all possibilities and you will be spellbound. Forever and always.

Yours are the magical wings on which I fly.

The seeds of yesterday

replaced with the promises of tomorrow.

Yet here we meet: right here, right now, forever in eternity.

You are blessed with my love

and I am blessed with your presence.

Together we will create unstoppable magic.

• PART THREE •

Hallowed

· 1 ·

Storms rise and fall, lovers enchant and divide, but all the while the one constant remains true: your integrity that is burrowed deep within. What is integrity, you ask? It is nothing more than the absolute conviction of what you were put on earth to do and remaining steadfast to that truth, in spite of storms—disastrous and many— and the platitudes of men who have come to praise you. For this praise is as disastrous as any storm, for here gives rise to your ego—the enemy of your conscience—and to here you will forever long to return.

But the true heart longs for no such praise; she longs only for the sweet satisfaction of fulfilling her purpose, finding her truth, and giving rise to her integrity. For integrity cannot live when the ego is on the lookout, constantly searching for the next victory.

Beware of victories, for in every victory lies defeat, and the one defeated is not always so clear. If you make an enemy of your own heart you will constantly be in battle, whether in the most peaceful surroundings or in the dark depths of your soul's torment.

Believe nobody when they sing your praises; believe only what you know to be true in the deepest glittering tunnel of your pure existence. All wonders, miraculous and true, require no such praise; they require only observation and reverence, reverence from which no words can speak.

Harbour no ill will towards those who seek to compete with you, for they too are trapped in the lower dimensions of their controlled minds.

Harbour only ill will towards yourself when you know that you should know better. Rise above this relentless suffering. This is the culture of self-debasement, and you will become more fulfilled every moment that you walk away from this psycho-attack that society places on you.

Praise does not bring you love, it brings only a wanton core of mass destruction. If you ask what is wrong with the world today, there lies your answer. A culture built on mass delusion is bound to be miserable, regardless of how fast you run from the inevitable.

Fear builds and builds in those seeking self-satisfaction, because all praise is fleeting, lasting only a moment before you are set adrift again, constantly longing to return to that false light, that brief moment of satisfaction. The hills of sorrow are built on the bodies of those engaged in this endless pursuit. Turn around and head not for these hills, but instead return to the ocean of your soul—an ocean of endless love that leaves no room for self-praise and false economy. Bury your trophies of these reminders and move towards a future free of judgment and self-recrimination.

This is where happiness lies, not in the heart of what society deems to be acceptable, beautiful, fashionable, or true.

The only truth that exists is inside of you, and this truth never builds on praise or artificial economies of the mind. This truth expands only with the light and not from some desperate need to be loved or admired by others, for this truth knows that it is loved beyond measure and longs for nothing but to be realized by you. Walk along these dew-covered fields and marvel at the beauty that lives within you, not outside of you. You are the light. You are love. You are forever. Any external source that does not acknowledge that is not worth pursuing. Waste not another precious moment—seek only to find your truth. Remember, time waits for no man.

. 2 .

Treasure the moments of silence you find under the golden stars, for there lies the portal to all places and all times. The stars are a gravity unto themselves, their deepest treasures bound by creation but hidden from view. Wherein lies monstrosity, one only has to gravitate towards the stars to be reunited with lost loves, truths so distant and yet so pure that they can be felt in an instant.

Your connection to the stars lies in the truth that you are created from the same substance that created the stars, the wind, and the earth. Your solitude, your endless longing, your deprivation, all stem from your misunderstanding of these key points. Look not to the stars to dream of faraway places; look to them to reunite with family, lost loves, and innate truths, for here can be found your essence, the soul seed of your creation.

These stars shine brightly for you, just as you shine brightly to further galaxies. Endure no misunderstanding, no separation from the origins of your source. Lie on your back and feel the earth beneath you and look to your heart above you, pulsing, pulsing, pulsing above you, beneath you, and within you. The heartbeat of creation is all around you, yet you are blind to its magnificence.

Look no further than the stars for everything that is beautiful and miraculous within you. Is one star more beautiful because it is larger? Is one star more alluring because it is more visible to the eye? Impossible! Such nonsense belongs not to the hearts of enlightened men but only to those who are walking through life blindfolded. Remove your mask, release your shackles, and burn brightly in the knowledge that a star burns within you, a star no more or less miraculous than those stars above you.

Imagine the day when every person on earth releases their light and removes the shackles of society's expectations. Earth will shine from afar, its light so paradoxical that ignorant men will fail to understand it, yet they will not deny it.

Caution applies to the road of the many, for this road is dotted with death traps, potholes, and dungeons of unspeakable horrors. The path of the free exists only for those who refuse to be burdened by the expectations of others. Release your fears, refuse to be judged, and wander carelessly into the light.

Heaven awaits, its light blinding and glorious, a light that can only be witnessed by the soul, for your feeble eyes are not capable of processing such magnificence. Such blinding force would devastate the strongest mind. Only the soul encounters it, but to describe it in the realms of the "seen" is to deny it its greatest truth, for its greatest truth is beyond such limited capabilities as the sense of sight.

HALLOWED

Treasure not what your eyes can see—move beyond such limited perception. Move into a place of such unequivocal brilliance that the brightest star seen only with the eye will look ordinary and plain. Accept that the universe's greatest beauties remain unseen, and begin your path towards the known, for what the soul experiences it knows, without need for reassurance or justification. Dungeons are crammed with men who refuse to walk this path. Trust me, as miraculous as a star is to the naked eye, this is only a miniscule compared to what awaits you. This I swear. Fear nothing, embrace everything, and search for your light within.

· 3 ·

Trouble arises when the heart is not free to meet its true desire. The heart wants not what the mind knows, but only what it knows to be true and earnest.

Sanctuaries exist within, yet your mind searches for them in the visible, in all corners of the globe. Travel far to find the light of your soul, but do not travel if your will is to escape yourself, for this is an impossible journey that will only end in misery.

HALLOWED

For the grandest holiday in existence, turn off all phones, quiet all noises, and cancel all distractions. Close your eyes and meditate on the sound of your beating heart, beating as one with all of creation. Let this beat take you into the silence—a silent splendor filled with pulsing stars, miraculous angels, and untold beauty. Here you will find a sanctuary that no other can measure and it will cost you naught. Don't despair the prices of so-called sanctuaries that offer nothing but the time for silence—make that time your own and you will need no guru, no amount of pampering, and no slaves to travel with you to your destination.

Stop right now: breathe, listen, release, surrender, conquer, paradise. This is your recipe for true and everlasting happiness.

I shall repeat myself no more, for I have sung the virtues of the silence within, the heartbeat of the universe, and the light of the many over and over. Now it's time for you to take your sword and wage war with your mind, for here lies the only true discovery. Resist not the temptation of your soul; resist only the temptation of your mind.

There I go, repeating myself when I had offered to stop! But some words bear repeating. It is only on incessant rotation that some words get through, and my message has certainly been incessant.

So remember: go within, find your light in the calm of the silence, and let it shine for all the world to see. You will do the world the greatest pleasure if you follow these simple truths.

· 4 ·

Love is not meant to divide but only to unite. Any division has no place to walk in love's name. Love embraces all things, accepts all things, believes all things. God knows only love. Do not live in the ignorant fear that this truth could be otherwise. Love is all-inclusive, always surrendering, and always nourishing. A love that does not nourish all that abide in the universe is not love at all. Remember that, next time you spout your false truths and hypocrisies.

To love is to care for all and to turn your back on nobody, for in your darkest hour you would pray that nobody turns their back on you. And I deem this to be true. Those who dare walk in my name make a promise to uphold kindness and the highest moral values that include all living beings. Ignore nobody in your search for love. Enslave only the highest moral virtues on your path to surrender.

Don't blind me with empty platitudes if you mean one thing but say another. I don't want you to live another day imposing your loneliness on others. Find peace in your heart and you will radiate peace to all around you, and then only peace will come back to you. This is the sanctuary of the Lord. This is the soul's home, where it longs to return, and where it's always been.

Eternity is bliss when it is Heaven that awaits. Hell lives only in the fear of men. Do not let it blind you from the beauty within—here is your sanctuary, here is your truth, here is your love everlasting.

Amen.

Love is the whisper of your soul

The valley of your heart

The bridge on which I climb.

How else can I guide you if not with love?

It is love that binds us

Love that carries us

And love that sets us free.

Doubt me not and I will be yours.

www.ingramcontent.com/pod-product-compliance
Lightning Source LLC
Chambersburg PA
CBHW020327010526
44107CB00054B/2004